for Mel & Doreen
with fond regards
& best wishes
Say.

Journeying

Sam Adams

First Impression—May 1994

© Sam Adams

ISBN 1 85902 146 8

All rights reserved. No part of this book may be reproduced, stored in a retrieval system, or transmitted in any form or by any means, electronic, electrostatic, magnetic tape, mechanical, photocopying, recording or otherwise, without permission in writing from Gomer Press, Llandysul, Dyfed, Wales.

Printed by
Gomer Press, Llandysul, Dyfed

Acknowledgements

The Anglo-Welsh Review, PN Review, Planet, Poetry Wales,
Aquarius, The New Welsh Review, Kibris.

Contents

POND LIFE

We've had problems with our pond.
First the lining wasn't right and water
Slid down the rubber lip, leaving
A muddy puddle where fish flapped
Derisively. Then the heron came
At dawn, before we were about to see
Its glide, low over hawthorn, its quiet
Splintering of reflected light, the squint
Before the sword fell. Three mud-coloured fish
Survived, to prove that glistering
Can be dangerous.

In autumn, after weeks of rain,
The garden moved and promised
To unload aubretia, pansies
And some nameless yellow stuff that wintering
Looks like tangles of waxed string,
With tons of mud, into our scrap
Of dark inverted sky.

That seemed unkind. The green hair
That hung about its eye so long
Had cleared at last. We hired Steve
To build a better wall, repair the mess
I'd made, see all secure.

Digging behind the old wall's sagging front
Unplugged the private homes of frogs,
That stood their ground inside their frog-shaped
Moulds, too dazed to shuffle off.

No wonder that last spring it seemed
We'd struck a well of freckled jelly.

I'd had to scoop the cataract
Of ooze away to clear a wink
Of early sun. And some survived,
Like muddy fish, and grew from dots
To frogs, hoppers cap-a-pie, smaller
Than my finger-nail, that took the air
Like us, turned up in grass
At mowing time, for reasons
Cornered in their shallow skulls
Refused to budge
When prompted to return to water.

Steve said they'd die in frost
And dropped them by another fissured wall,
Trusting they'd see the dark and squeeze inside.

There are lessons here.

Look after walls when soil turns mud
And heaves down slopes. Life's certainties
Are often undermined, and hope
Can vanish under avalanche and flood.

Beware of predators with beady eyes
Who get up early. No matter how refined
They may appear, they'll gulp you down:
A little common earth is good disguise.

Small loves can burrow underneath the skin
And grow in there, make fattening their career.
If some sharp blade exposes them to frost,
Show them a chink and let them crawl back in.

PLOUGOULM TO ROSCOFF

A monstrous tide daily separates
Surprised sunbathers from their scorching cars,
And with meticulous care
Parcels acres of sand and river-bank
In crisp green wrapping,
Textured like hand-made paper.

Swelling the brook as far as the café
Au Pont de Bian, it is greeted
With customary thoughtfulness
By anglers squatting on the low stone walls.

Inside, workers from the neat fields gather.
One curses the French:
—*Chinois* they call us, Chinese, he bellows,
Swallowing a final glass of wine.
He has an *affaire*—with his wife, he explains,
As waving and weaving he cycles off
On this last night before the Johnnies sail.

Midnight, in Roscoff, close to old harbour walls,
A grey mist of dust rises
From the feet of lines of dancers,
Arms linked, stepping the most restrained
Of folk shuffles. Old airs and instruments
Carry far over still black water,
Like a sheet of plastic, barely wrinkled.
But the Breton sea is imperceptibly receding,
And behind the tranced eyes of young dancers
Another tide is going out.

THE OLD HOUSE

Just here it is easy to close the eyes
And see dancing aunts and a maudlin butcher,
A cage of banisters, windows
Where seeds or spores like heaps of tiny coins
Trickled in at crevices, meaningless marks
On a bedroom wall, a pianist and a small boy
Who turns the pages as she, smiling, nods.

THE PIANO

We had talked of selling the piano,
But suddenly there was an unplanned space
Where after-images persisted
That filled both ear and eye—
The children side-by-side before the keyboard,
Log-jams of repetition that kept us busy
In the kitchen, the gradually less grudged
Yielding of a tune. I burned the broken
Music stool with autumn sweepings
Whose smoke merged slowly into dusk.

THE TABLE

Polishing the table from the old house,
I marvel at the spell that turpentine and beeswax
Hold over wood, and see dimly in the grain
The face of someone I once knew—
Though not nearly well enough.
And yet he's there. And that first breath
After chapel he was somehow mingled with the air,
I recollect, that clogged my throat.
We shall eat together at this table
And scarcely ever feel a hand's reflection
Warmly grasp our own.

THE GARDEN

Last evening till the gnats bit and again
This afternoon, I killed (Caradoc's word)
My grass. Not hay but tangled couch,
Resistant to my hook's unnatural stroke.
From the pungent shadow of the elder
To the withy's drooping fan, I have crouched
Above my victim like a crazy lover, until its green
Stained my knees and fingers and my back
Was crooked as my hook. And what's achieved?
A ragged waste that tells me
I can have my way, and count the cost.

HELSINKI

More than the sum of its myriad parts,
Nature resumes old outposts in the streets:
Bunched rocks washed to a pink glow
And lilac weighting the air
With unseasonable spring.
Finlandia's ghost looms low
Among its trees and Mannerheim
Is riding to the east, that loaded question,
A seagull on his hat.

At midsummer the city has its share
Of birds of passage—duck and grebe,
Ourselves, other confused songsters
Cheapening their morning ritual
By rehearsal through the daylit night,
And sundry fellow-travellers.
Having made its point, the rain persists
Unreasonably on drenched red plumage
And bedraggled chants.

From Olympic Quay
A ferry bound for Leningrad
Slides seaward, is erased by mist...
But like a palimpsest persists,
Uneasy after-image on the mind.

ELK
(for Sue)

Uffe built his summer-house
On Trutoren, close to the shore
Where long reeds grew. Before he came
Elk possessed the spot. Creatures of habit,
They still appear at the edge of the clearing
And look down long noses
At the furious dog.

In high summer they move at dawn,
Traversing the densest thickets
Like a whisper. Following trails
They laid long before the metalled road
Was made, they sometimes loom
Before the headlights like vast, substantial
Spirits of the woods. Butchered there,
They crash across the buckling steel
To take the hapless driver with them.

Elusive, they can stand so still
In swampy moss among the trees
Skilled hunters will pass by them.
Conjure now the elk of dreams—
Hugely bulked against the twilight,
Palmate antlers like sails full-spread,
Wading in pools to drink, feasting
On lily-pads.

            Goitered and shaggy
Aristos on stilts, they must have watched
While, midge-bitten to the knees,
We blundered by on Trutoren.

HILL FORT, CAERLEON

From this tree-finned hill
Breasting the breeze—
Leaf shadows like water shifting,
Sounds of water always moving
In the preening of so many leaves—
I can look down over old Caerllion.

In the aqueous rush of bracken fronds
Breaking round, and in a sound
Clearer now, once heard,
An unbroken hum
Like some instrument endlessly strummed
On one low note, or the tone

Of wires looped from pole
To pole vibrating through wood
Where we pressed our ears,
There is a sense of something living,
Breathing, watching here
As I push towards the rampart mound.

The path is blocked. A swarthy
Sentry bars my way; his spear-
Tip sparks with sunlight.
He challenges in accents I know well;
The words I recognise but the sense eludes.
I am ashamed and silent. He runs me through.

CAERLEON TO LAMPETER

Days of rain from a shale-coloured sky,
Slanting over foundations of ancient barracks
And new villas. Water gathering
Relentlessly in yards and roadways,
Dripping from hedges. Abergavenny,
And already bridges closed by flood,
Diversions. An early dark
Swishes round the wheels,
Wipers cut clean sectors
From the blur and first headlights
Decline politely to the right.
In a deeper darkness the hulk of the bannau,
Like an upturned prow, drives into the drenched gale.

Few other travellers care to navigate
These roads on such a night.
My own cone of light and the white lit
Road unwinding unhinge the mind.
Three signs advance and, bowing to the beam,
Announce that men are working
(At this time, in such loud weather?),
The road will narrow and snake beneath my wheels.

But these are incidentals.
The whole of Wales is awash
In the night. Near Pumpsaint
A new brook flows across the road. As in a dream
A rat swims easily downstream, his eye
Glimmering in the headlights' glare.
Into Llanbedr, and the sheen of lamplit streets
Assures me others have survived.

JEFFERY LLEWELYN

Looking for Prichard, I found the church
Bleaching in the sapped autumnal sun.
As I lifted the latch, chill led me
By the fingers to the rapt inside.
With hum of trapped bee or weary fly
For company, and the rustle of turning pages
Like the uneven hiss of failing breath,
I saw all the Prichards and Pritchards of Tŷ Mawr
Rise up in their generations and fall again to dust.

And after Trallong, the same quest in stone places,
With traffic sounds a century distant
And footsteps on gravel filling the interstices
Of years, numbly fumbling
Among the families of hosiers and glaziers,
Fishermen and farmers and their wives,
Their acknowledged children—and the others . . .

March 31st Averina reputata filia of Thomas Prichard
     was baptised
November 1st John reputed son of David Prichard
     was baptised

What goings-on between those sheets.

How can you forget a man
With a false nose and an 'earnest snuffle',
Encumbered with those hopeless books
Like Christian with his load of sins?
Haunter of theatres, gaunt buttonholer,
I see you sometimes still
At the edge of vision, turning a corner
At the far end of a terrace
Or just swallowed by a mist.

Tone-deaf minstrel, through all your travels
Some sad fate tracked you—even to World's End.
Did that wax prosthesis drip with anguish?
What irony to afford a fire at last,
And burn you in it.

MARTINS' NEST

In the old shed, high up, much magnified
And lit by sunlight gay with dust,
A martins' nest, like half an acorn cup

Or a clay blister plastered to the rafter,
And the parent birds gleaming in stippled
Rays like blue-black flames, then swallowed

Without trace in the scaled and roughcast cyst.
Despite the ladder's awkward stance, I climbed
Among rods of sun impelled through rusty pores

Rotted in the thin roof's corrugations
Slanting pencil-thick to the oily floor,
Solid enough to my light-fingered touch.

A crusted chalice growing from the beam
Descended slowly to my upraised eyes;
Though my young feet fumbled rungless spaces

My giant head rose by the lip.
In spontaneous combustion of feathers
The fledgelings fled, their wingbeats scattering

Through the falling shed; I remember
The ladder reeling and my father's shout
Slicing the sunbeams before the light went out.

THE WOMAN ON THE SWING

After tennis on long summer afternoons,
Sweating, salt on the lips, eyes wincing,
Heat along the thighs, we would watch
The cool woman on the swing.

She lazily swung a full, easy curve,
Rising with her legs thrust straight,
Falling back on the arc, knees bent,
Rising and falling in abandoned trance.

Her blonde hair streamed, a comet's tail,
Charged with portents, then wrapped its gleaming
Tendrils round her cheeks and closed eyes,
As she scooped back through the eager air.

Even now I cannot reconcile
That image with those frantic blows
That sent her blood in fountains
Up the wall where she fell dying.

HUSBAND AND WIFE

They never walked together—
The beast with his branded face
And brutish glare always strode ahead,
She, plain and cowed, meekly walked behind.

So might their way be now,
But one night she took the heavy gun
And, while he slept, blew half his head away.
Launching him bloodily into the void.

RUNNER

He had a portly poise and duckfoot walk
And butler's backward leaning stance,
But also the unnerving trick

Of almost instant disappearance.
For Bob Wilkins loved to run,
Could as a ponderous old man

Raise a surprising gallop
Even going up
The steepest shabby terrace—

Wyndham Street or Maesteg Row
Or Tramroad Side—to dodge the law;
Beneath a memorably dirty coat

Voluminous and long, like a battered bell,
His greased boots scudded up the hill.
And Bob's clients liked the race he

Always gave them for their money,
On the flat or over the sticks,
Till the Gaming Act stopped him in his tracks.

YOUNG BOB

Bob in his careless, idle youth
Felt with his hands an inner strength—
Beneath the serge and supple skin,
The pause and flick of muscles as he ran.

He loped with his greyhounds,
Scaring silvered sheep
From dew-wet bracken fronds,
Leaving the valley to its man-haunted sleep.

And on warm days, by the red and white striped shed,
Dreaming winners, clocking pigeons' rings,
He whirled a lasso of grey birds round his head
And coolly sat amid the turbulence of wings.

AERIAL MANOEUVRES, POWYS

From their hillside in the south
Of paradise ascending buzzards
Find that spiral crystalline
And idly plane on air as pure
As perspex. Hail the morning
In the north of paradise,
From Llanfihangel
To Llanfyllin! Limpet
Nests lift from the tide beneath
The eaves. Full morning: swifts
Strafe crowded streets, bouncing
Off slabs of sky, shrilling
At each ricochet. A high jet
Slowly scrapes a fingernail
Across the blue and others,

Flying low, abort the stock
And frighten children.
In the senseless blare of metal
Our small world of human gestures
Shrinks to the merest blur
Of red and green. This sunlit
Morning death rehearses
The final rending of the vale.

CATS' CRADLE

My mother's chair had wheels;
Her skinny arms grew big with moving it
From the bedroom to the kitchen,
Round the house and back again.

She did her gardening by proxy,
Sitting in the doorway in the sun.
While she watched she knitted,
And the two cats lay still
Among the coloured skeins
That decked her lap.

If nothing grander was on offer,
Like dancing or a day out at the races,
This is how she'd wish it:
A sunlit doorway, two contented cats
And busy fingers, an everlasting, neat
And weed-free garden.

AGHIOS NIKOLAOS TO KRITSA

All foundations here are sound
(As Minos thought, before the earthquake struck),
You build your home upon the mountain's cobbles
Or blast a house-sized hole into the rock—
After the puff of dust, a muffled thump,
There is no compromise,
And then the whiff of cordite.

New routes are blasted too,
Each with its quota of surprises:
Confrontations at blind corners,
Shrines at the apices of bristling hairpins,
Momentous glimpses of peaks, ravines and sea.

The road is as pitted and contorted
As the olive trunks that line it.
Within the bus the women's voices chime
Above the grind and rattle of a low-gear
Climb. The strange terrain
Exudes from its rocks and pungent herbs
A comforting smell of human sweat.
Perhaps we would do well to heed
Its peace, follow ancient paths,
As patient as meditation, with room enough
For an exchange of simple words.

But the motor keeps its promise
To deliver us on time to this village
Clenched in the old way to its crags.
We feel an urgent thirst we have not earned,
Find shade beneath a plane tree's awning,
Drink deep, at the portals
Of another language unlatch our feeble tongues.

SLIDING

Do you remember the ritual of candle wax,
The lanes of rubbed grass pale-gold like flax?
Do you remember how we used to slide,
Sharing the cardboard, down the mountainside,
You with your slim girl's thighs spread wide
Accommodating my narrow loins? Your hands
Held fast my summer shirt,
And when the ride began
You pressed your head against me hard
And bit my shoulder till it hurt.

Do you recall the gasping flight
As the cardboard swished down the narrow track?
There were jarring bumps when your legs clung tight,
And I thrilled
At your light cries,
Though I couldn't see for the dust in my eyes.
Too soon, to soon, the final thump
Left us sprawled and stilled
At the foot of the tump.

ROUGH BOYS

Their father played the banjo,
Squatting on the doorstep in his pitclothes,
Dancing his steel-tipped boots
On a dirty patch of pavement.
And their brand of bullying was perversely merry,
That to dream of the rough and ragged brothers
It not quite a nightmare.

Now in the bar those furies
Of my past are grown to manhood
And have paradoxically shrunk.
Their swaggering and tarzan cries
Are only in my memory.

They sold the banjo when the old man died:
A stone fell on him my father said.
The death I saw was neat,
The body carried whole up from the dark.
Years afterwards I heard the monstrous weight
The mountain shrugged on him.

BIRD STRIKE

In the spring I watched the earthbound
Creatures nesting, tending no young,
Coming and going;
I heard sounds of their living,
The mingling of unmusical voices.

They worked the garden too,
But could not know each leaf and stem
As I do. I saw them mock
My dewfall pantomime,
My scrutiny of wormcasts.

With summer came the yearning.
I skimmed mahonia beads, marked
My beaten bounds
With purple patches; but still
My airy girdle chafed, and still

Their closed world beckoned. No-one
Saw my near approach, my chattering
Glide. I seized the moment
When the blue door opened wide,
And crashed into the clear sky inside.

KITE FLYING

On days of noisy wind that combs
The rippling grasses this way and that
As it passes, and tugs at clothes

With sly unbuttoning fingers
And takes the breath away, I think
How we would lie in some drowned hollow

While the slow kite wriggled in its stream.
How sad that some boys never learn
To fly a kite. I thought that I

Should never get it right—perhaps
I had made my cross too rigid,
Perhaps my paste and paper were too frail.

We knew those moments when the breeze
Would fail our fledgling project
And the taut-held line would sag,

But we launched out sweetly on the air
Again and cast off twine enough
To let our hobby climb and climb.

RENOIR AT 'LES COLLETTES'

I love the olive trees, my grove;
I shall not leave this place. I nurse
These bandaged roots that once were hands,
Suffer at unshuttered windows
The limp embrace of gauze curtains,
Bibbed like an infant or aged
Imbecile am mute at table.
Dribbled wine like thin blood streaks
My beard; I regret the company
Of friends. Who breaks for me my bread?

Who tends my sores? Who wipes my eyes?
It is not easy to outface
The sidelong mirror. Taut as primed
Canvas, my skin stretches over
Prow-sharp beak and bony orbit.
The old gnarled pain pulls like a knotted
String through arteries and veins.
What am I but boneyard litter,
Dust for the winter winds of Midi
To sift into a sunny corner?

Antithesis of flesh, I worship
Ripeness still: plump fruit, the juice-full
Forms of women. Yearning towards them
With my clamped brush, I dissolve them
Into light, like an addict drink them.
I love the olive trees, my grove,
The glamour of this dappled garden.
I shall never leave this place.

THE RENOIR FAMILY AT ESSOYES

On the spit of noon the village trembles,
Liquefying in its bowl of heat.
Along the river bank where Renoir walked
Poplars ascend from small black pools.
Awnings hang still. The stripes of vineyards
Hatch the stony slopes to dry plateaux.

The cemetery's other visitors
Lay their wreath to 'Ménager—mon grandpère'
With tributes from 'ses amis et voisins',
Old soldiers and ex-prisoners of war.
The shells that edge this path
Are from no sea-shore of the world.

Renoir's gaze seems fixed upon the road
The panzers must have rolled along;
His famous sons are with him.
Behind them watches Aline Victorine,
Much like life. Shading her broad
Burgundian face she wears a hat—
As we, had we been wiser, should have done.

FIRE AND WATER

Here in my hot attic room—
The window open, books strewn,
Birdsong and a hint of woodsmoke—
I think of Shelley, naked
In his tower of glass.
The sun of Tuscany has focused
To a white heat in his brain
That keen, enraptured freedom
Of the soul and senses.

Then, as some blots of cloud,
Like petty tyrants and mad despots
All endlessly renewed,
Smudge the dull orange
Of a gathering storm,
I see the long-limbed body
Rolling slow, the eyes wide,
Unflinching in the purest blue,
And the fish begin to gather.

KYRENIA SHIPWRECK

(About 2300 years ago, a trading vessel plying along the coast of Anatolia and among the offshore islands, sank off Cyprus, about a mile from what was to become the port of Kyrenia. The wreck with its cargo was found by marine archaeologists in 1967.)

The old man and his sons had little hope,
They sank with the ship.
The gods reserve another fate for me.
It was the firewood I cut on Rhodes
That bore me up until the squall
Had passed, and then I blessed the skill
That poverty had taught:
The fatherless dive for sponges on Ophioussa.
Again I swam to stay alive.
The north-west wind that herds
The waves ashore brought me safe home.

I know this sea—its salt has made me deaf.
I know rising through it to the light,
Air spent, the ring of rocks and sand,
The mountains veiled with mist.
I know the fish, have been one with them
While breath allowed, have watched the coinage
Of their evening circle of the bay.
If any man can cook them sweeter
Let me shake him by the hand.

We ate well for traders. I flung the net,
They sometimes helped me draw it in.
We put ashore with firewood and cauldron
And I would bake the fish in leaves
And stir the white flesh fallen from the bones
With a little oil and almonds;

And then good olives, goat's milk and cheese,
And carobs, and a beaker full of wine.

Wine was more than half our business.
We loaded amphorae on Samos,
Four hundred more on Rhodes.
From Cos we bore two dozen
Corn mills carved from basalt
And the almonds packed in jars.

The old man's beard was white,
And the ship had been his father's.
The hull of resinous Aleppo pine,
Repaired a thousand times, was sound
He said, because it wore a skin of lead.

Weighty too it seemed to me.
I thought the load had grown so great
A little sea could wash aboard,
And so it proved.

We reefed the sail, the two dead boys
And I, and stowed it in the stern.
The old man's wisdom was perhaps at fault,
But our courage did not fail;
It was the ship surrendered to the sea.

I crawled upon the sand with wits intact;
My strength soon mends. But I am poor again,
And who will take to sea a man
Whose luck outlasts his master's.

DIPPING

Mid-morning it appeared,
Staining the mountain like a liquid,
Spreading unpredictably,
And against the law of nature
Sometimes uphill and across,
But inexorably to the farm,
Where it rolled and eddied
Like scummy water stirred.

The first signs were the shouts
And whistles and the endless
Bleating that's the repertoire of sheep:
Baa—I am disturbed.
Baa—I do not like this.
Baa—Where are you?
Baa—I'm lost.

Old ewes and well-grown lambs
From the dungy yard sprawl
In the reeking dip, scramble out
And gallop off. In thirty feet
They stop to graze, trauma forgotten.

Early evening and the flocks
Are scattered seeds, pearl barley
On the darkening slopes, or strung
Like beads along their old high paths.

DUBLIN TO DRUMCLIFF

Jolting westwards,
A muffled landscape wheels past,
Till a dramatic wand of sunlight
Clears carriage windows
To reveal multitudinous greens.
Then Roscommon, and ragged hedges
Give way to grey walls
That seem designed to fix a field for good.
Some hold fine harvests of tall weeds,
Or flocks of starlings on the boil;
One full of lumpish stones
As though old walls came there to die.

From Ballymote a shock of mountains
Crest on crest, great nobs of green
Encrusted with outcrops and streaked with scree.
The track recoils in a wide curve.

Sligo at last, late afternoon:
A long procession of men following
A flag-draped coffin, talking quietly,
As though this was the most mundane
Of reasons for a stroll—a salute to old heroes.

I parade my self-sufficiency
Along the road to Drumcliff.
It is tea-time for tourists, the churchyard empty.
I pay my respects to an old hero, footsore,
Wish I had a horse to take me back.

THE SYNGE EXHIBITION

The bird he mounted and his butterflies,
A receipt from Dublin's Naturalists' Club,
The solitary sceptic's violin;

A Paris diary, precise, in French,
Noting, in December, 1896—
'Fait le connaissance de W. B. Yeates.'

His camera, a brown box, beady-eyed,
And the careful sepia photographs he took—
The Macdonagh cottage on Inishmaan,

Aran's shawled women and bonneted men,
Their baskets and nets on Kilronan quay.
Letters from friends in beautiful Gaelic.

His slanting spidery hand at speed,
And an unbelievable typewriter—
'Will you go into the little room

and stretch yourself a short while on the bed.
I'm thinking it's destroyed you are
walking the length of that way in the great rain.'

Outside a heavy sky presses the roofs;
Clean rain persists, but with a whiff of Liffey
My drenched coat drips on the library floor.

LIVERPOOL TO NEWPORT

Beneath its shell the station seethes;
Its shade hums. Weary at setting forth,
Travellers tug their luggage
Past no entry signs to switched platforms.
Trains are running late.

Through open windows we receive
The sibilants of burning rails,
The in-drawn gasp of speed through cuttings,
Backwash on pebbled shores.
Connecting doors are wide to show
The train's long tunnel snaking
With the track. We are inside
A bitch's tail, that slowly wags.

A conveyor load of varnished landscapes
Winds by, courtesy of British Rail:
Grain's for once true gold, spun out,
Long stems of seeding grass, dark hedges
And dry ditches.

              Beyond Gloucester, a haze rises,
And heat has ironed out the Severn's creases.
Verdigris and gilt, the river bends
With the track's bright steel. Past Chepstow
Into Gwent, I start the countdown
Of villages and landmarks to the station,
The car park and the short, hot drive—and home.

THE POND REVISITED

In early spring I saw the heron once,
By chance, juggling a fish to swallow.
The movement of the curtain was enough
To spread those great grey wings
Over the inky scribble of the hedge.
But he'll be back. He breakfasts early
And leaves a milky calling-card.

Fish make few demands
And feeding them is cheap.
Not so heron. The heron's alchemy
Transmutes to ordure gold and silver.